kumił
design book

Name: _____

Date: _____

Notes

#	Braid	Date
1		
2		
3		
4		
5		
6		
7		
8		
9		
10		
11		
12		
13		
14		
15		
16		
17		
18		
19		
20		

#	Braid	Date
21		
22		
23		
24		
25		
26		
27		
28		
29		
30		
31		
32		
33		
34		
35		
36		
37		
38		
39		
40		

#	Braid	Date
41		
42		
43		
44		
45		
46		
47		
48		
49		
50		
51		
52		
53		
54		
55		
56		
57		
58		
59		
60		

#	Braid	Date
61		
62		
63		
64		
65		
66		
67		
68		
69		
70		
71		
72		
73		
74		
75		
76		
77		
78		
79		
80		

#	Braid	Date
81		
82		
83		
84		
85		
86		
87		
88		
89		
90		
91		
92		
93		
94		
95		
96		
97		
98		
99		
100		

Notes:

Braid Name: _____ **#** _____

Colors _____

Beads _____

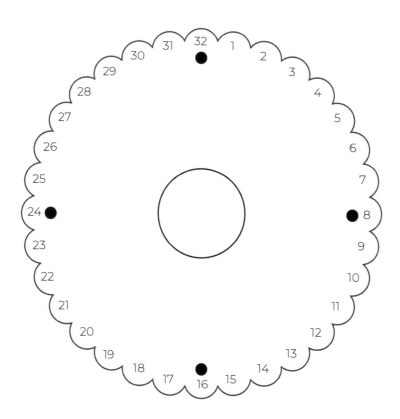

Moves:

Notes:

_____
_____
_____

Braid Name: _____ # _____

Colors _____

Beads _____

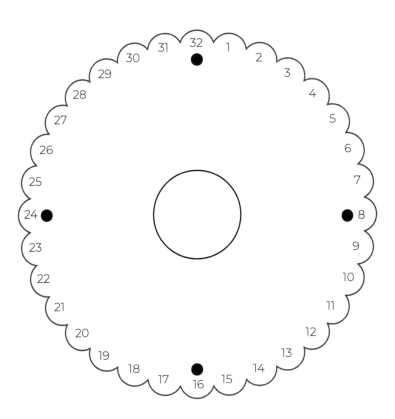

Moves:

Notes:

_____

_____

_____

Braid Name: _____ # _____

Colors _____

Beads _____

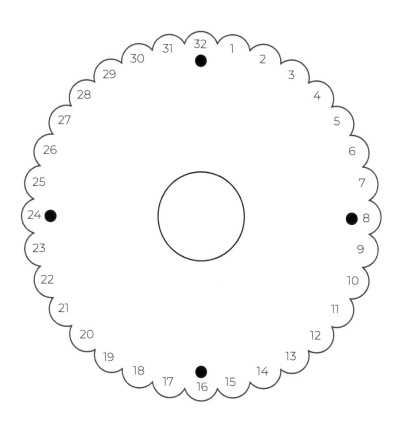

Moves:

Notes:

_____

_____

_____

Braid Name: _____ **#** _____

Colors _____

Beads _____

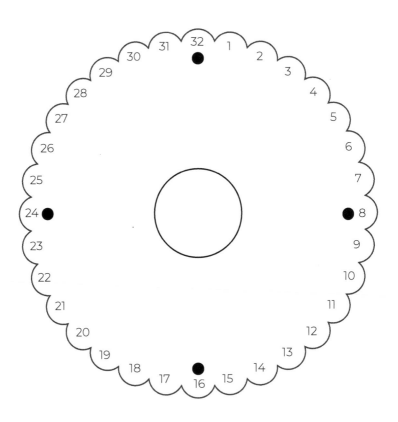

Moves:

Notes:

_____

_____

_____

Braid Name: _____ # _____

Colors _____

Beads _____

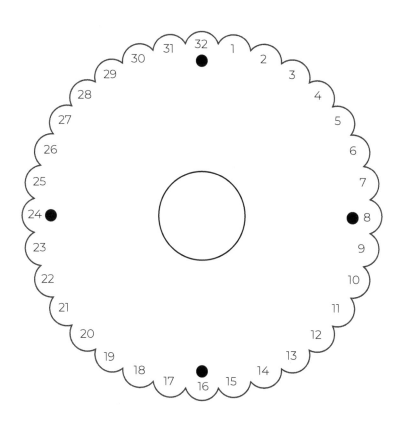

Moves:

Notes:

_____

_____

_____

Braid Name: _____ # _____

Colors _____

Beads _____

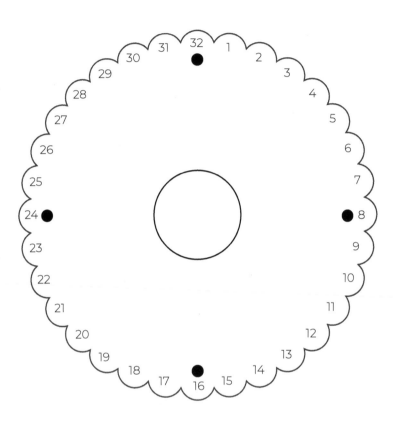

Moves:

Notes:

_____

_____

_____

Braid Name: _____ # _____

Colors _____

Beads _____

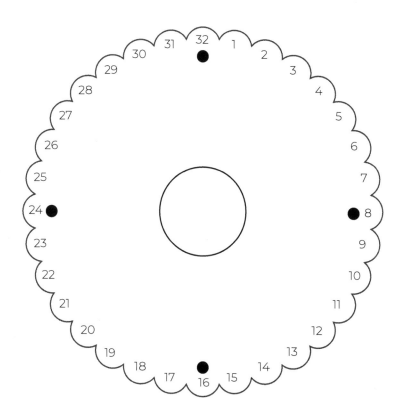

Moves:

Notes:

_____

_____

_____

Braid Name: _____ # _____

Colors _____

Beads _____

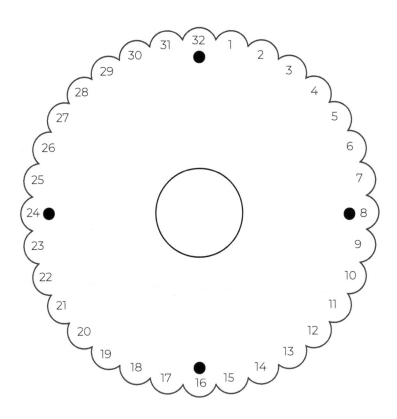

Moves:

Notes:

_____

_____

_____

Colors _____

Beads _____

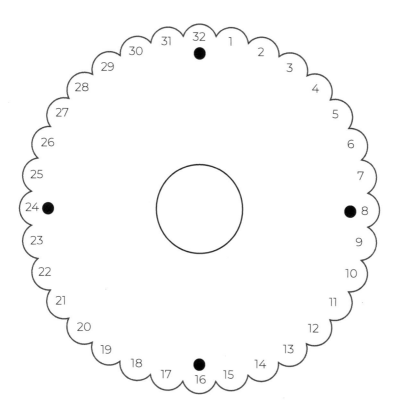

Moves:

Notes:

_____

_____

_____

Braid Name: _____ # _____

Colors _____

Beads _____

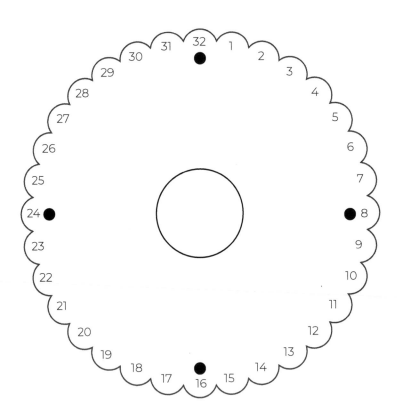

Moves:

Notes:

_____

_____

_____

Braid Name: _____ # _____

Colors _____

Beads _____

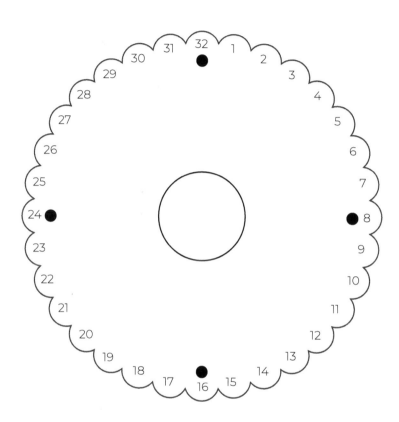

Moves:

Notes:

_____

_____

_____

Braid Name: _____ # _____

Colors _____

Beads _____

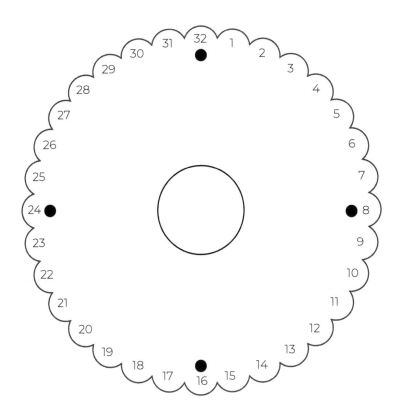

Moves:

Notes:

_____

_____

_____

Braid Name: _____ # _____

Colors _____

Beads _____

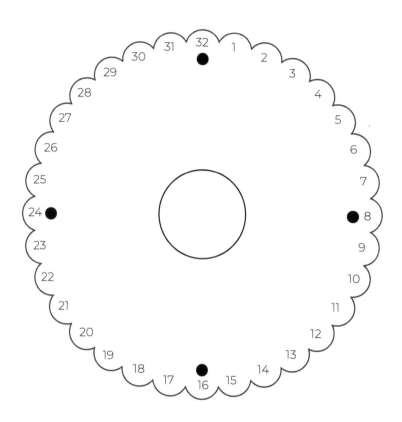

Moves:

Notes:

_____

_____

_____

Braid Name: _____ **#** _____

Colors _____

Beads _____

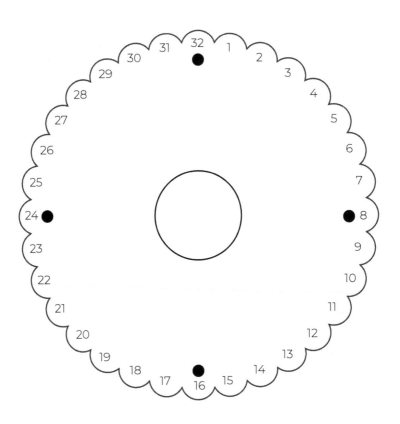

Moves:

Notes:

_____

_____

_____

Braid Name: _____ # ____

Colors _____

Beads _____

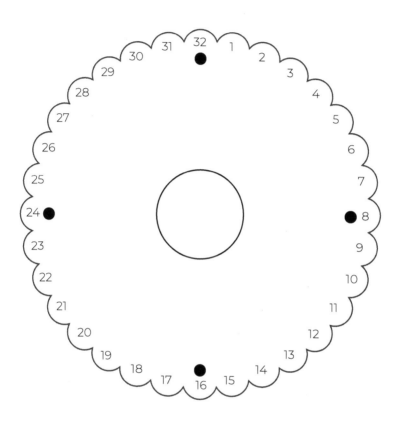

Moves:

Notes:

_____

_____

_____

Braid Name: _____ # _____

Colors _____

Beads _____

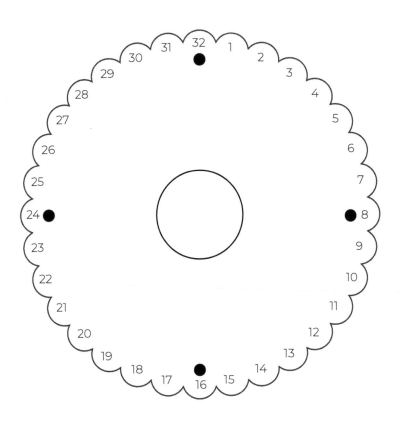

Moves:

Notes:

_____

_____

_____

Braid Name: _____ # _____

Colors _____

Beads _____

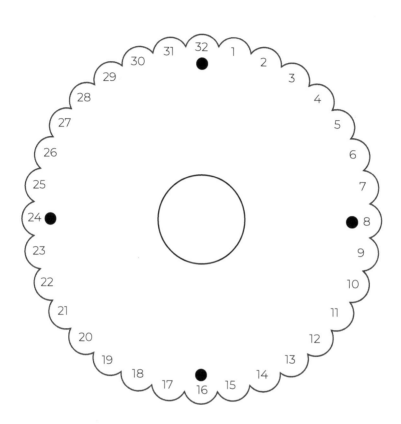

Moves:

Notes:

_____

_____

_____

Braid Name: _____ # _____

Colors _____

Beads _____

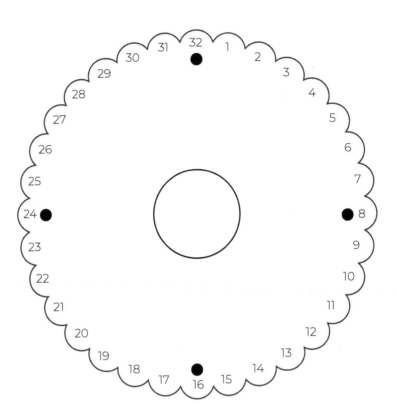

Moves:

Notes:

_____

_____

_____

Braid Name: _____ # _____

Colors _____

Beads _____

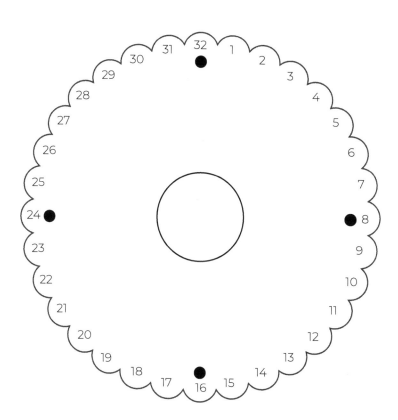

Moves:

Notes:

_____

_____

_____

Braid Name: _____ # _____

Colors _____

Beads _____

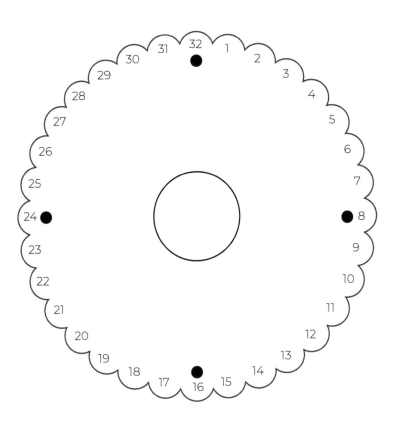

Moves:

Notes:

_____

_____

_____

Braid Name: _____ # _____

Colors _____

Beads _____

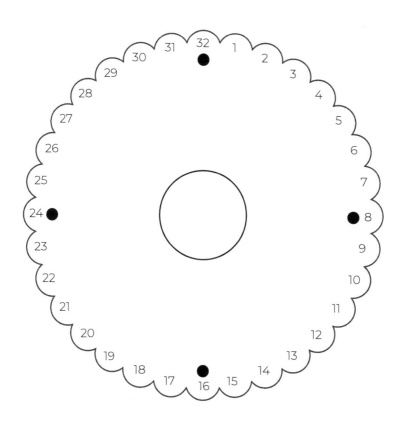

Moves:

Notes:

_____

_____

_____

Braid Name: _____   # _____

Colors _____

Beads _____

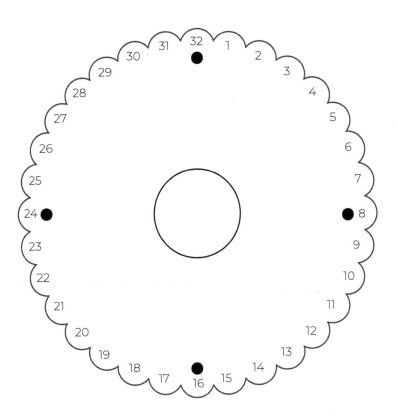

Moves:

Notes:

_____

_____

_____

Braid Name: _____ # _____

Colors _____

Beads _____

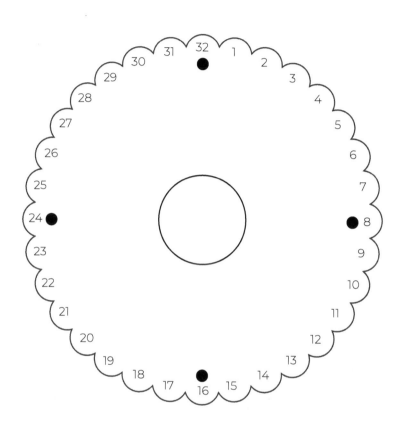

Moves:

Notes:

_____

_____

_____

Braid Name: _____ # _____

Colors _____

Beads _____

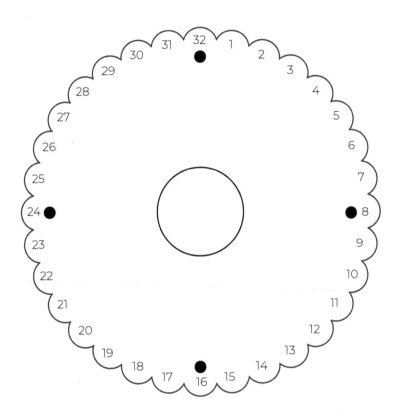

Moves:

Notes:

_____

_____

_____

Braid Name: _____ # _____

Colors _____

Beads _____

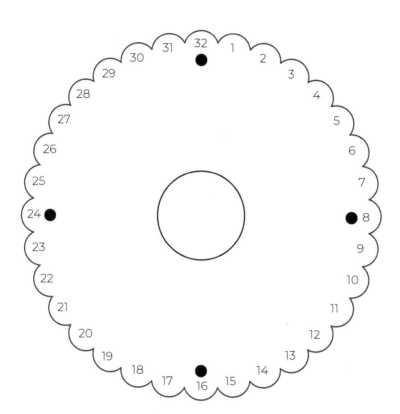

Moves:

Notes:

_____
_____
_____

Braid Name: _____   # _____

Colors _____

Beads _____

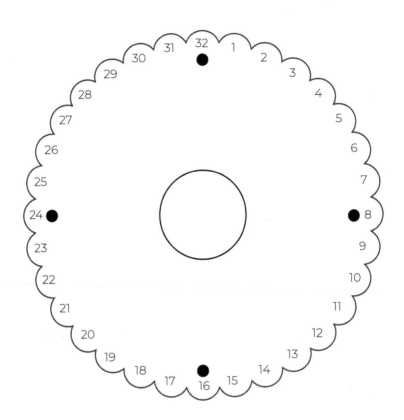

Moves:

Notes:

_____

_____

_____

Braid Name: _____ # _____

Colors _____

Beads _____

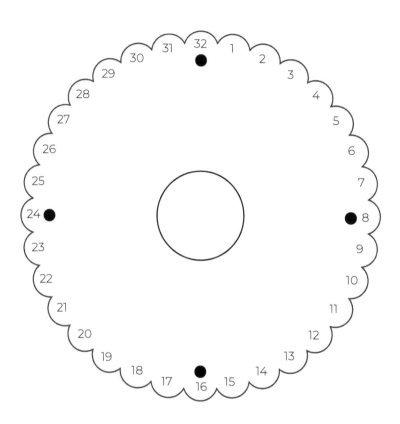

Moves:

Notes:

_____
_____
_____

Braid Name: _____ # _____

Colors _____

Beads _____

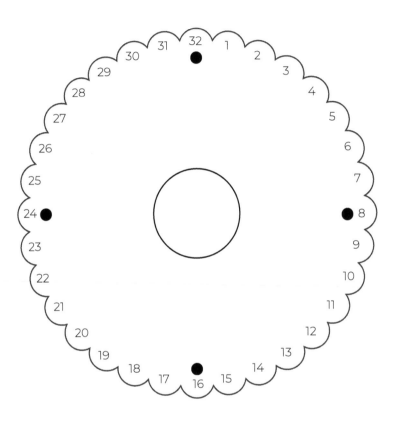

Moves:

Notes:

_____

_____

_____

Braid Name: _____ # _____

Colors _____

Beads _____

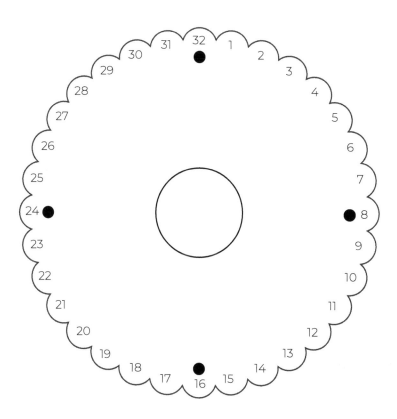

Moves:

Notes:

_____

_____

_____

Braid Name: _____ # _____

Colors _____

Beads _____

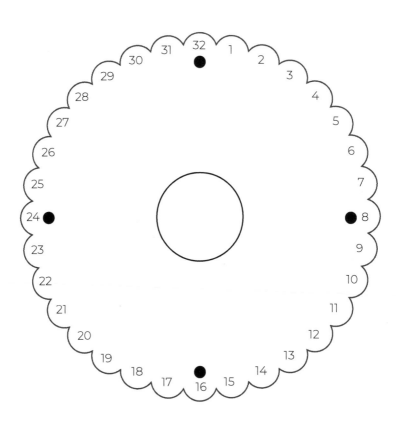

Moves:

Notes:

_____

_____

_____

Braid Name: _____ # _____

Colors _____

Beads _____

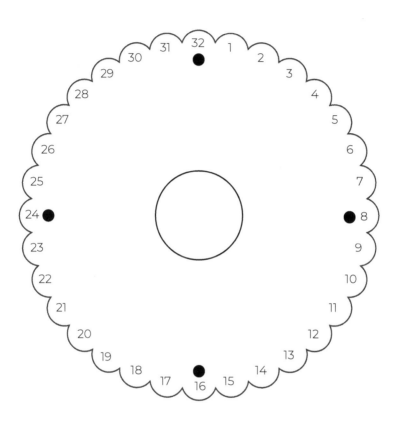

Moves:

Notes:

_____
_____
_____

Braid Name: _____ # _____

Colors _____

Beads _____

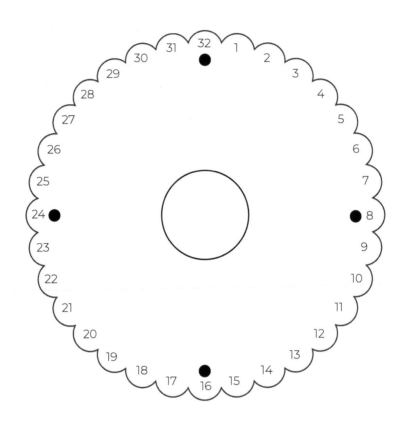

Moves:

Notes:

_____

_____

_____

Braid Name: _____ # _____

Colors_____

Beads_____

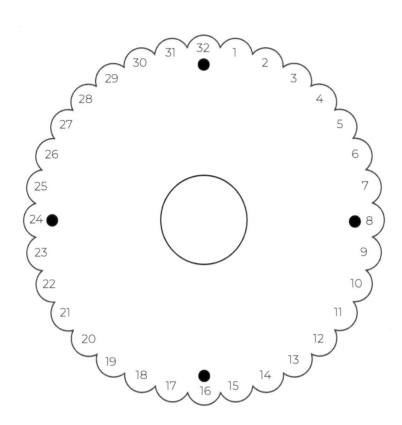

Moves:

Notes:

_____
_____
_____

Braid Name: _____ # _____

Colors _____

Beads _____

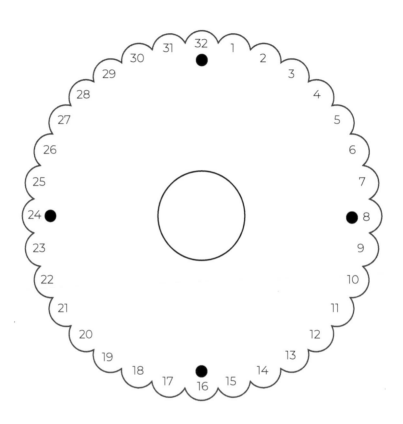

Moves:

Notes:

_____

_____

_____

Braid Name: _____ # _____

Colors _____

Beads _____

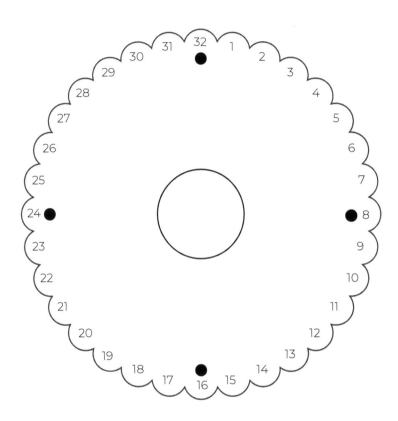

Moves:

Notes:

_____

_____

_____

Braid Name: _____ # _____

Colors _____

Beads _____

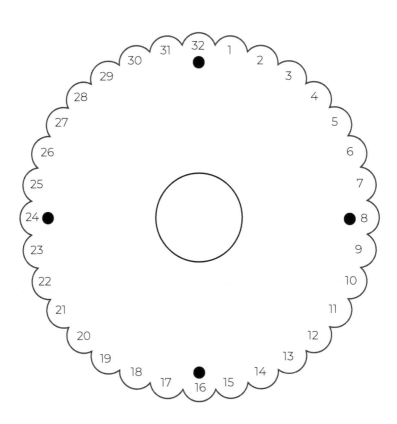

Moves:

Notes:

_____

_____

_____

Braid Name: _____ # _____

Colors _____

Beads _____

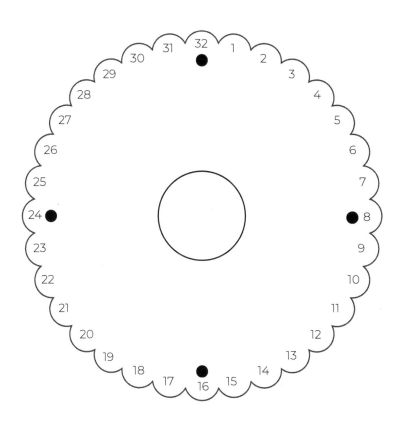

Moves:

Notes:

_____

_____

_____

Braid Name: _____ # _____

Colors _____

Beads _____

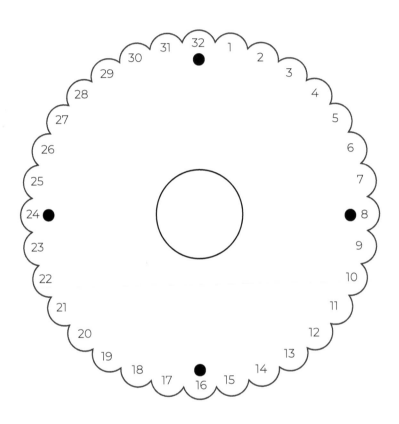

Moves:

Notes:

_____

_____

_____

Braid Name: _____ # _____

Colors _____

Beads _____

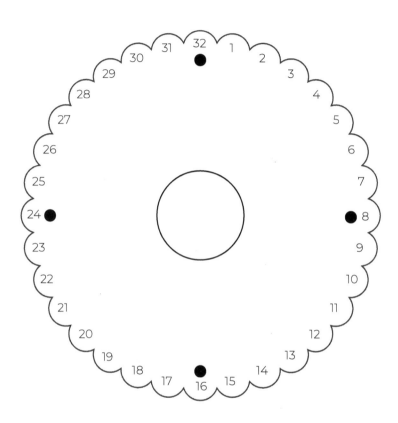

Moves:

Notes:

_____

_____

_____

Braid Name: _____ # _____

Colors _____

Beads _____

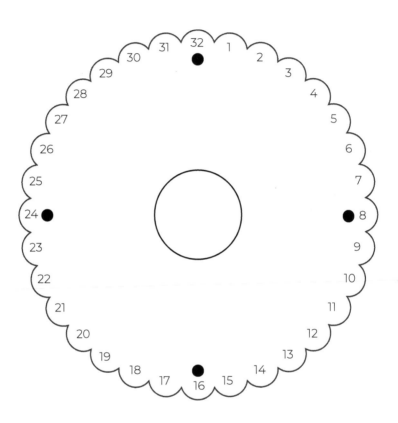

Moves:

Notes:

_____

_____

_____

Braid Name: _____ # _____

Colors _____

Beads _____

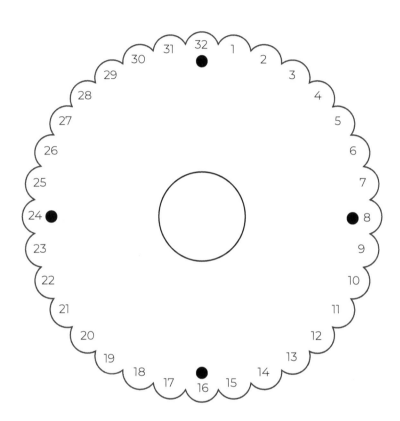

Moves:

Notes:

_____

_____

_____

Braid Name: _____ # _____

Colors _____

Beads _____

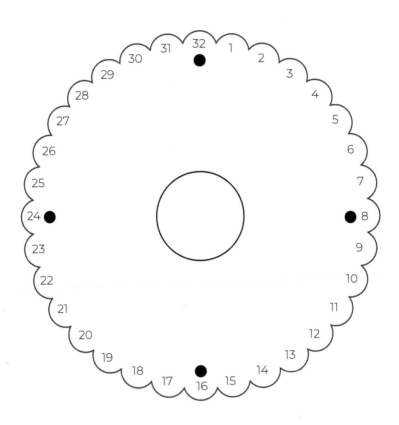

Moves:

Notes:

_____

_____

_____

Braid Name: _____ # _____

Colors _____

Beads _____

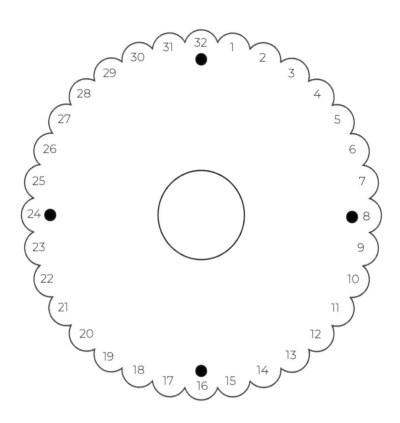

Moves:

Notes:

_____

_____

_____

Braid Name: _____ # _____

Colors _____

Beads _____

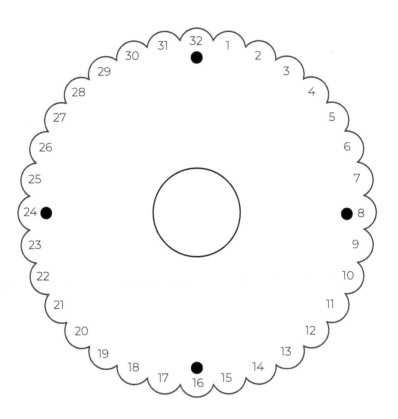

Moves:

Notes:

_____

_____

_____

Braid Name: _____ # _____

Colors _____

Beads _____

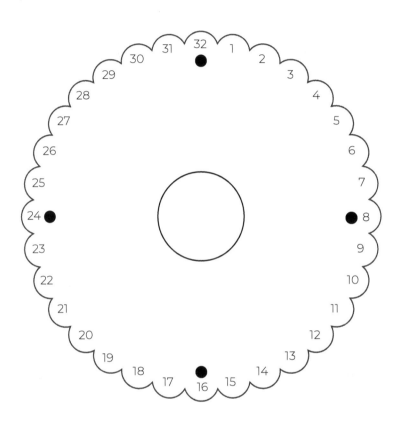

Moves:

Notes:

_____

_____

_____

Braid Name: _____ # _____

Colors _____

Beads _____

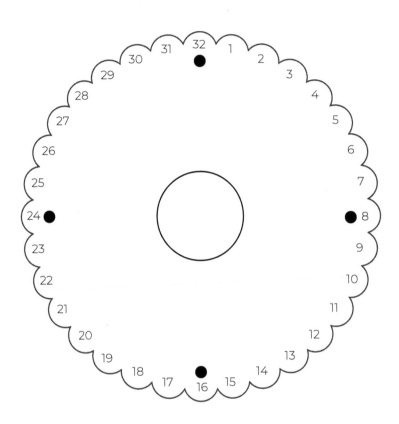

Moves:

Notes:

_____

_____

_____

Braid Name: _____ # _____

Colors _____

Beads _____

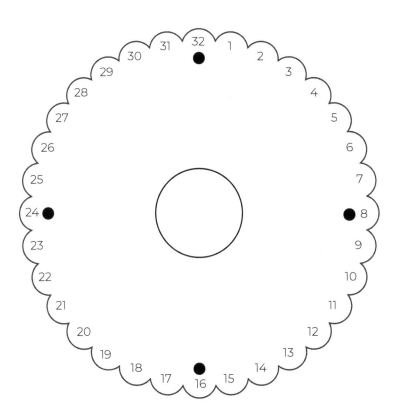

Moves:

Notes:

_____

_____

_____

Braid Name: _____ # _____

Colors _____

Beads _____

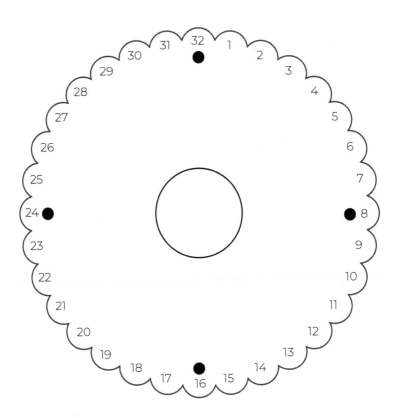

Moves:

Notes:

_____
_____
_____

Braid Name: _____ # _____

Colors _____

Beads _____

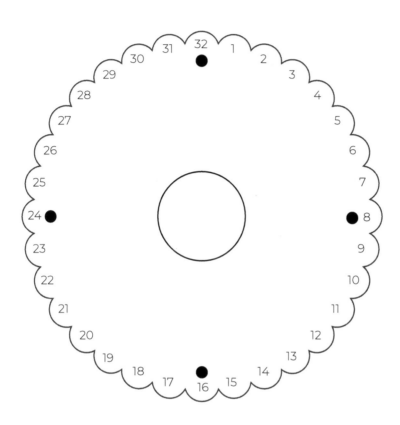

Moves:

Notes:

_____

_____

_____

Braid Name: _____ # _____

Colors _____

Beads _____

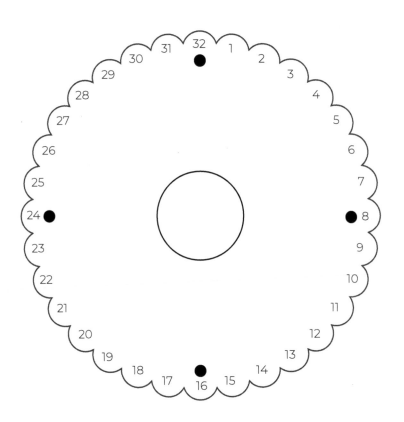

Moves:

Notes:

_____

_____

_____

Braid Name: _____ # _____

Colors _____

Beads _____

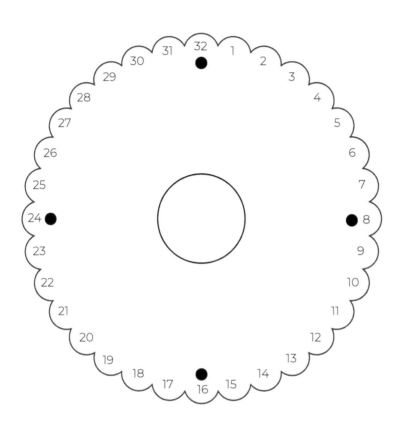

Moves:

Notes:

_____

_____

_____

Braid Name: _____ # _____

Colors _____

Beads _____

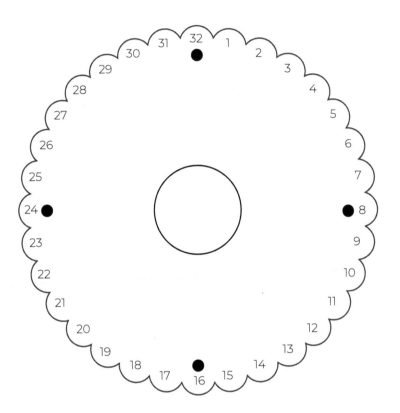

Moves:

Notes:

_____

_____

_____

Braid Name: _____ # _____

Colors _____

Beads _____

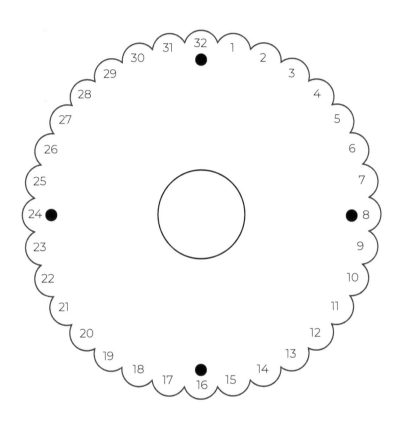

Moves:

Notes:

_____
_____
_____

Braid Name: _____ # _____

Colors _____

Beads _____

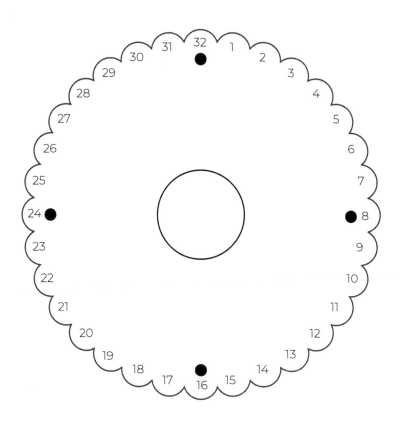

Moves:

Notes:

_____

_____

_____

Braid Name: _____ # _____

Colors _____

Beads _____

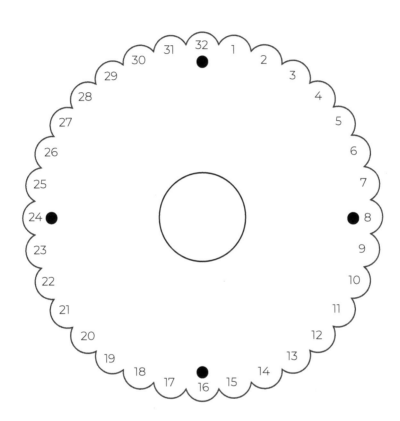

Moves:

Notes:

_____
_____
_____

Braid Name: _____ # _____

Colors _____

Beads _____

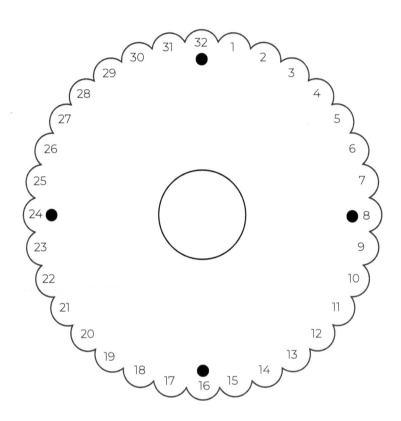

Moves:

Notes:

_____

_____

_____

Braid Name: _____ # _____

Colors _____

Beads _____

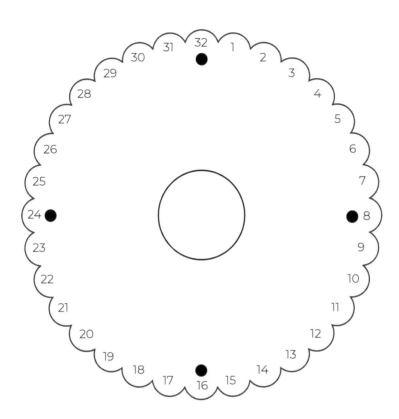

Moves:

Notes:

_____
_____
_____

Braid Name: _____ # _____

Colors _____

Beads _____

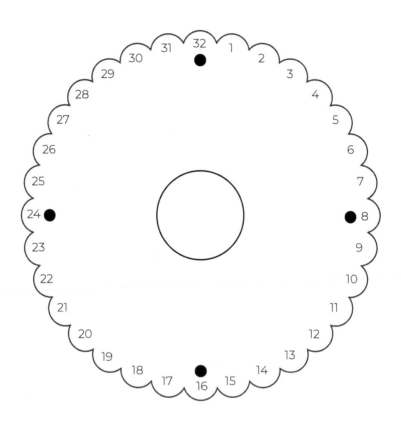

Moves:

Notes:

_____

_____

_____

Braid Name: _____ # _____

Colors _____

Beads _____

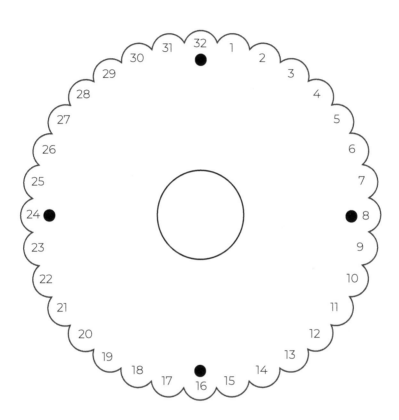

Moves:

Notes:

_____

_____

_____

Braid Name: _____ # _____

Colors _____

Beads _____

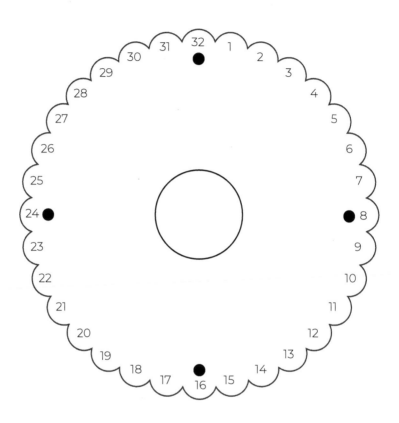

Moves:

Notes:

_____

_____

_____

Braid Name: _____ # _____

Colors _____

Beads _____

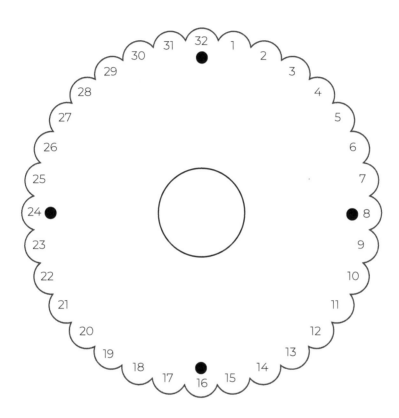

Moves:

Notes:

_____

_____

_____

Braid Name: _____ # _____

Colors _____

Beads _____

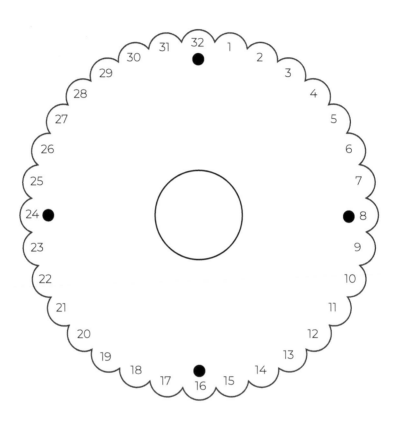

Moves:

Notes:

_____

_____

_____

Braid Name: _____ # _____

Colors _____

Beads _____

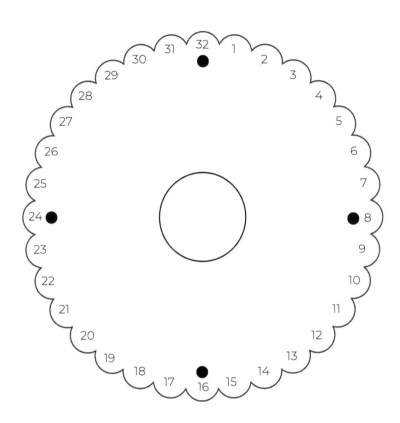

Moves:

Notes:

_____

_____

_____

Braid Name: _____ # _____

Colors _____

Beads _____

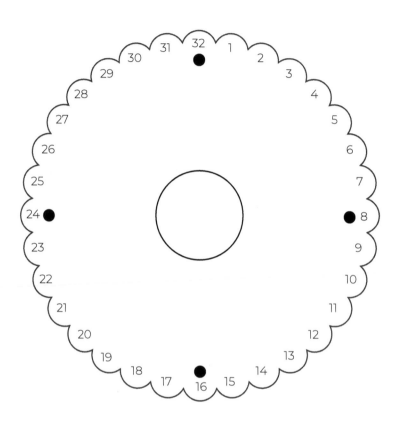

Moves:

Notes:

_____

_____

_____

Braid Name: _____ # _____

Colors _____

Beads _____

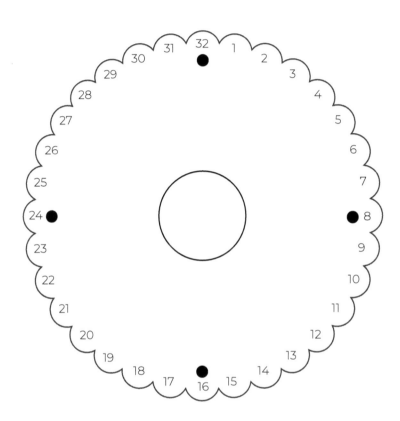

Moves:

Notes:

_____

_____

_____

Braid Name: _____ # _____

Colors _____

Beads _____

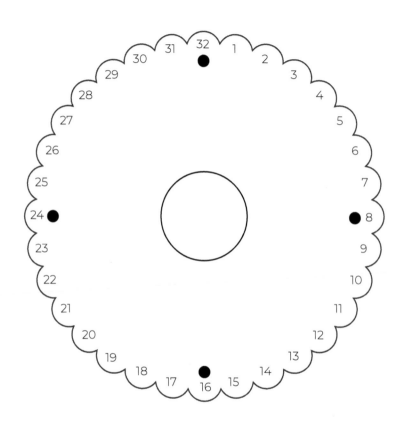

Moves:

Notes:

_____

_____

_____

Braid Name: _____ # _____

Colors _____

Beads _____

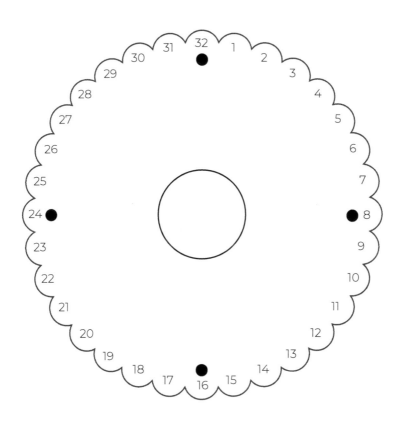

Moves:

Notes:

_____

_____

_____

Braid Name: _____ # _____

Colors _____

Beads _____

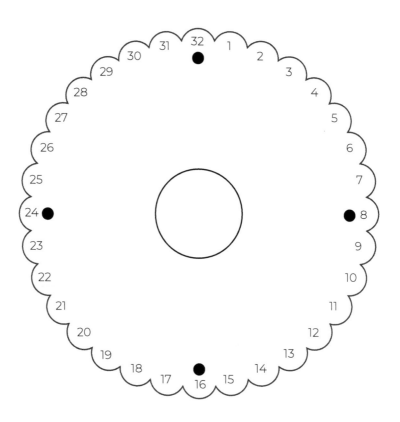

Moves:

Notes:

_____
_____
_____

Braid Name: _____ # _____

Colors _____

Beads _____

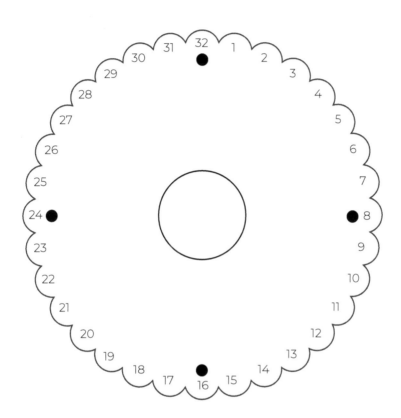

Moves:

Notes:

_____

_____

_____

Braid Name: _____ # _____

Colors _____

Beads _____

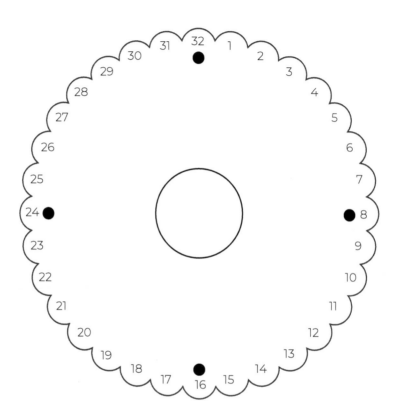

Moves:

Notes:

_____
_____
_____

Braid Name: _____ # _____

Colors _____

Beads _____

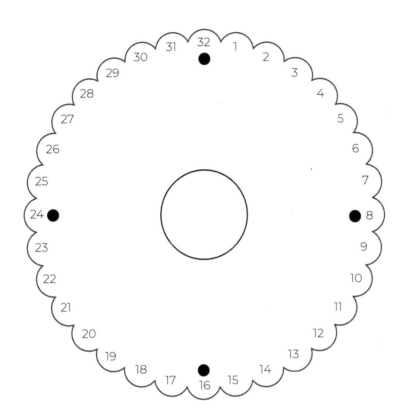

Moves:

Notes:

_____

_____

_____

Braid Name: _____ # _____

Colors _____

Beads _____

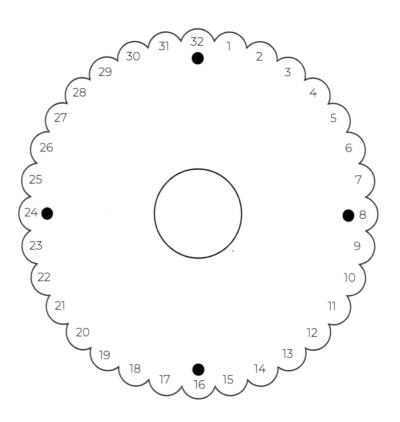

Moves:

Notes:

_____
_____
_____

Braid Name: _____ # _____

Colors _____

Beads _____

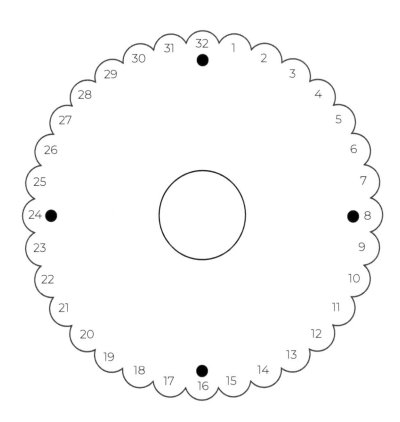

Moves:

Notes:

_____

_____

_____

Braid Name: _____ # _____

Colors _____

Beads _____

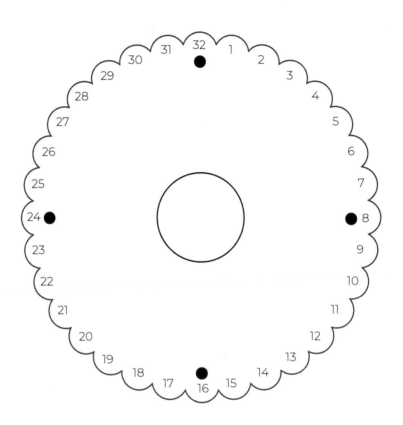

Moves:

Notes:

_____

_____

_____

Braid Name: _____ # _____

Colors _____

Beads _____

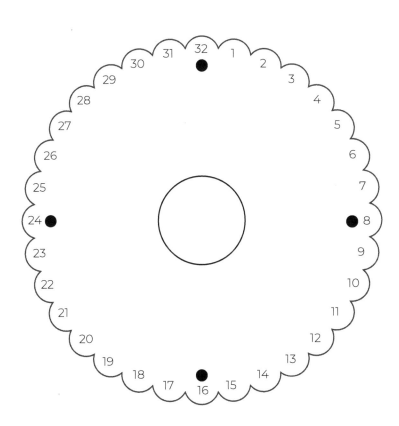

Moves:

Notes:

_____

_____

_____

Braid Name: _____ # _____

Colors_____

Beads_____

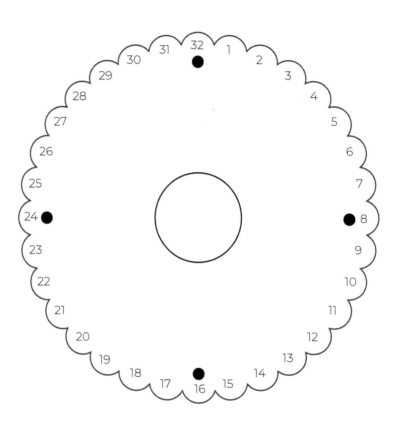

Moves:

Notes:

_____

_____

_____

Braid Name: _____ # _____

Colors_____

Beads_____

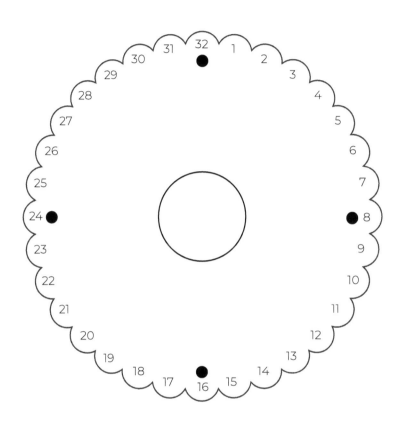

Moves:

Notes:

_____

_____

_____

Braid Name: _____   # _____

Colors _____

Beads _____

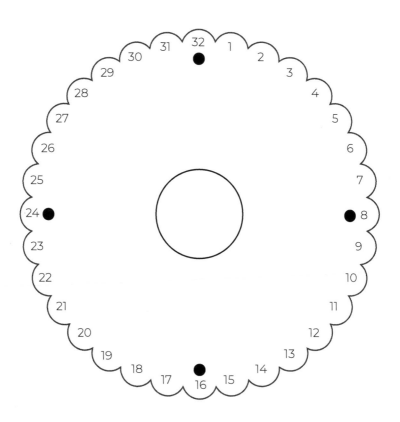

Moves:

Notes:

_____

_____

_____

Braid Name: _____ # _____

Colors _____

Beads _____

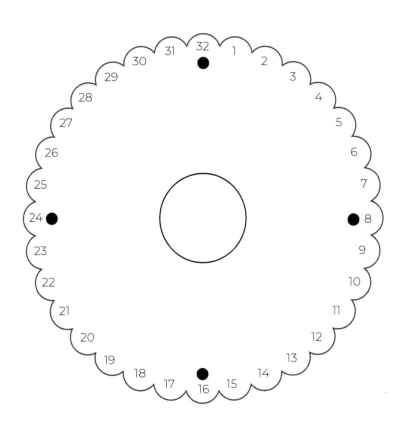

Moves:

Notes:

_____

_____

_____

Braid Name: _____ # _____

Colors _____

Beads _____

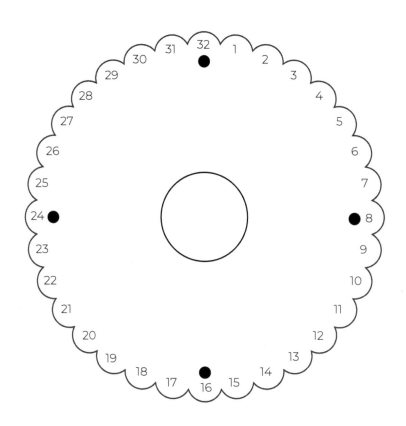

Moves:

Notes:

_____
_____
_____

Braid Name: _____ # _____

Colors _____

Beads _____

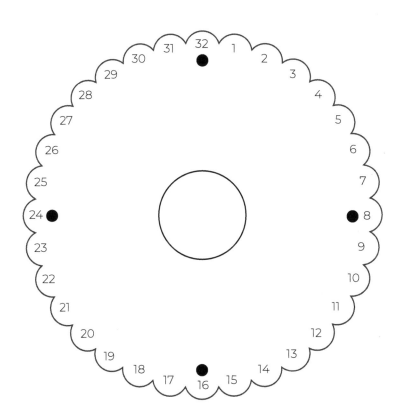

Moves:

Notes:

_____

_____

_____

Braid Name: _____   **#** _____

Colors _____

Beads _____

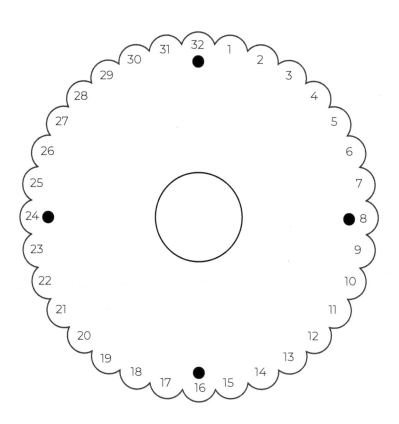

Moves:

Notes:

_____

_____

_____

Braid Name: _____ # _____

Colors _____

Beads _____

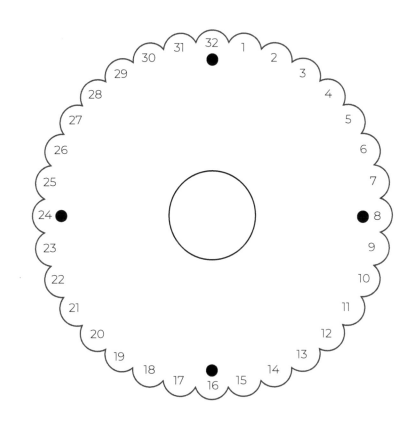

Moves:

Notes:

_____

_____

_____

Braid Name: _____ # _____

Colors _____

Beads _____

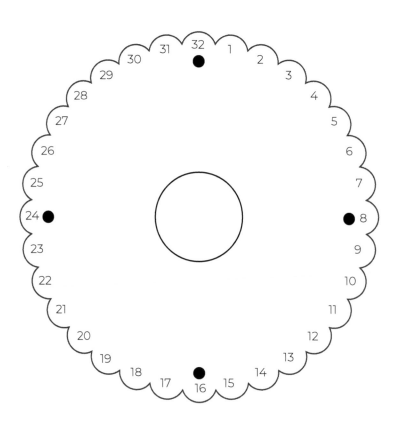

Moves:

Notes:

_____

_____

_____

Braid Name: _____ # _____

Colors _____

Beads _____

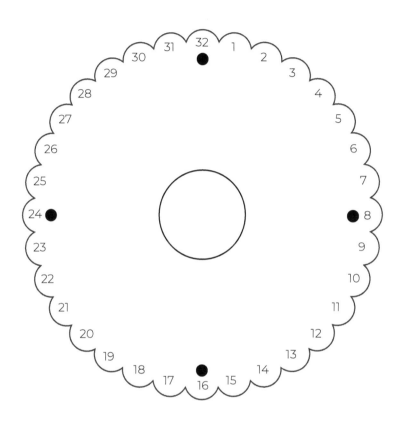

Moves:

Notes:

_____

_____

_____

Braid Name: _____ # _____

Colors _____

Beads _____

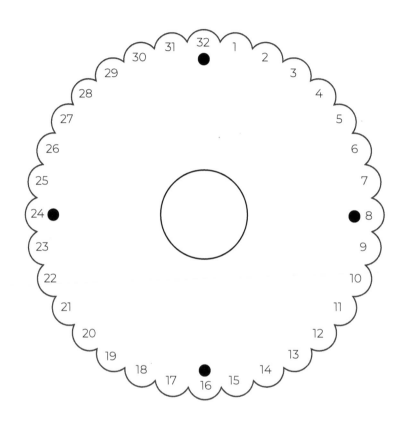

Moves:

Notes:

_____

_____

_____

Braid Name: _____ # _____

Colors _____

Beads _____

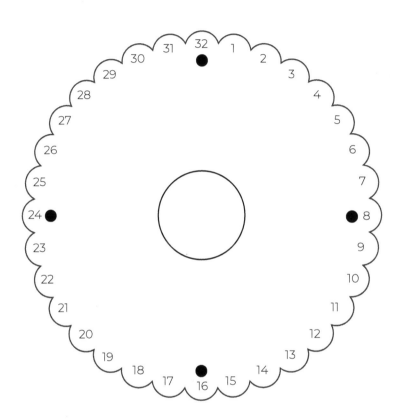

Moves:

Notes:

_____

_____

_____

Braid Name: _____ # _____

Colors _____

Beads _____

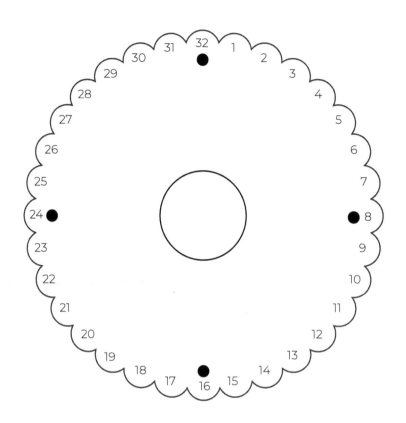

Moves:

Notes:

_____

_____

_____

Braid Name: _____ # _____

Colors _____

Beads _____

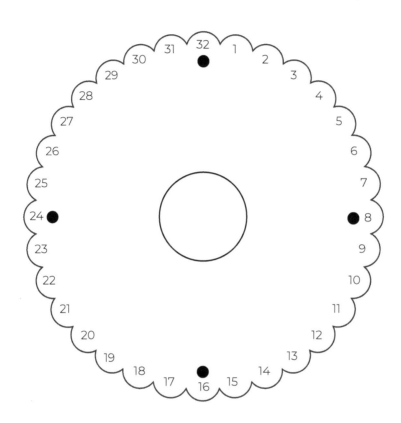

Moves:

Notes:

_____

_____

_____

Braid Name: _____ # _____

Colors _____

Beads _____

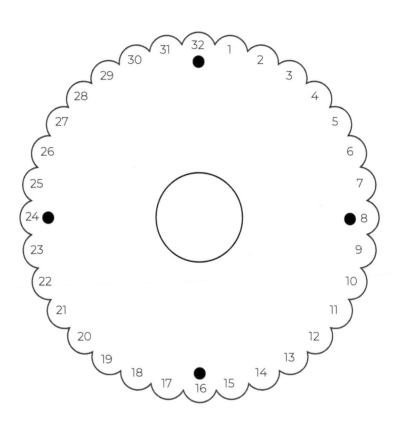

Moves:

Notes:

_____

_____

_____

Braid Name: _____ # _____

Colors _____

Beads _____

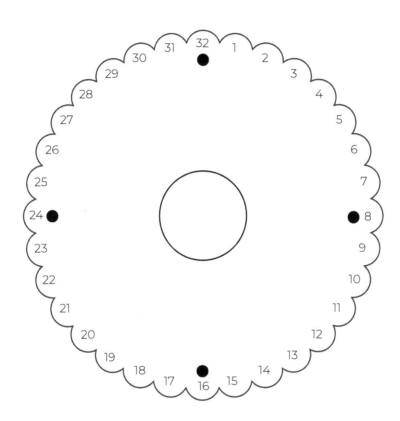

Moves:

Notes:

_____

_____

_____

Braid Name: _____ # ____

Colors _____

Beads _____

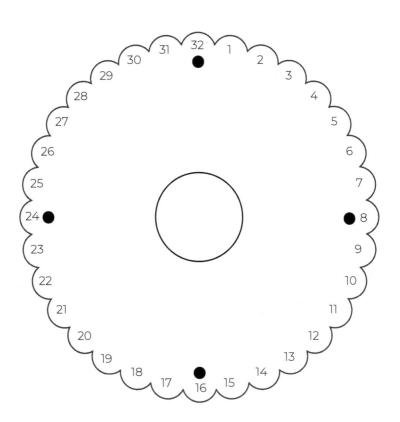

Moves:

Notes:

_____

_____

_____

Braid Name: _____ # _____

Colors _____

Beads _____

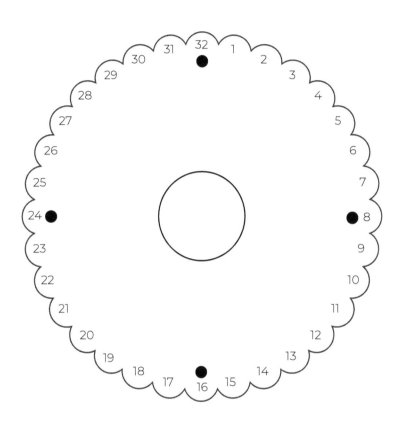

Moves:

Notes:

_____

_____

_____

Braid Name: _____ # _____

Colors _____

Beads _____

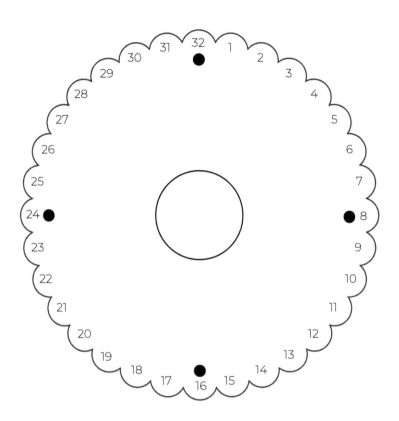

Moves:

Notes:

_____

_____

_____

Braid Name: _____ # _____

Colors _____

Beads _____

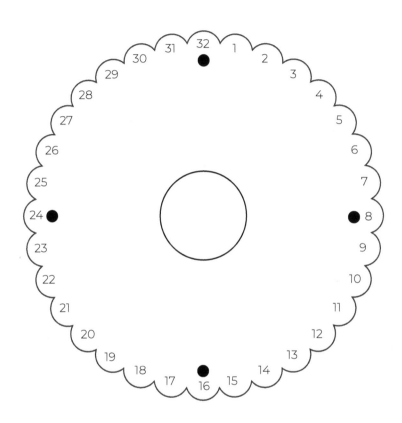

Moves:

Notes:

_____

_____

_____

Braid Name: _____ # _____

Colors _____

Beads _____

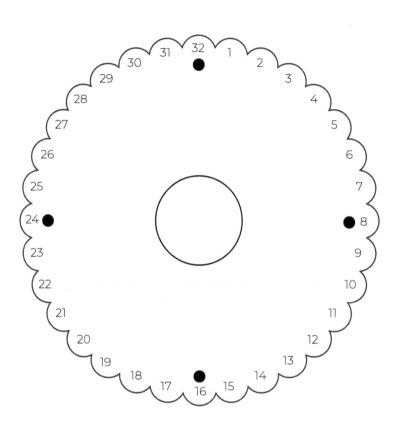

Moves:

Notes:

_____

_____

_____

Braid Name: _____ # _____

Colors _____

Beads _____

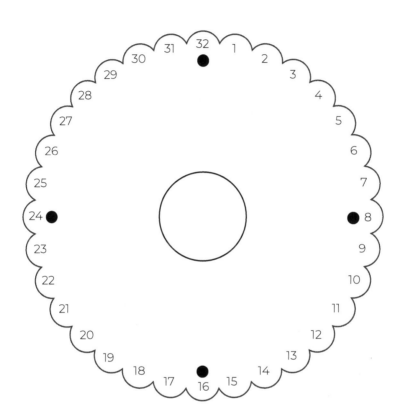

Moves:

Notes:

_____

_____

_____

Braid Name: _____ **#** _____

Colors _____

Beads _____

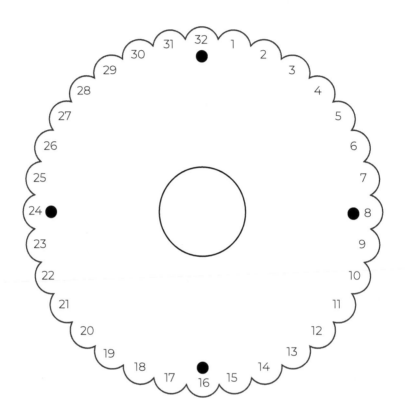

Moves:

Notes:

_____

_____

_____

Braid Name: _____ # _____

Colors _____

Beads _____

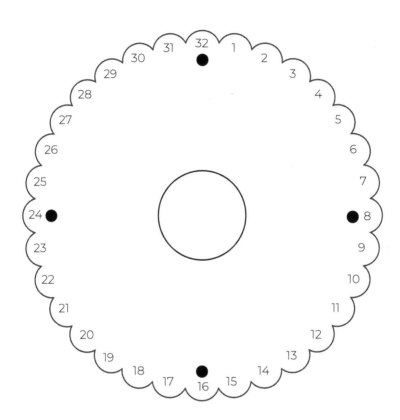

Moves:

Notes:

_____

_____

_____

Braid Name: _____ # _____

Colors _____

Beads _____

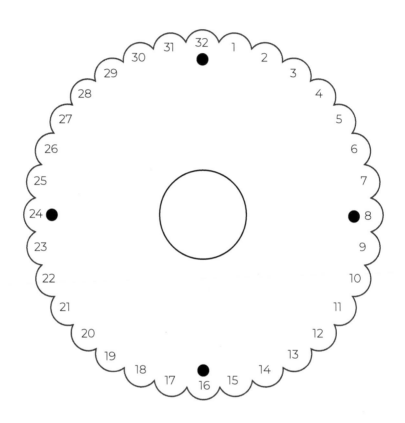

Moves:

Notes:

_____

_____

_____

Notes and Sketches